Bailey the Bear Needs Help!

Needs Help!

A True Story of Rescue and Rehabilitation

by Christy Gove

PUBLICATIONS
Adventure
an imprint of AdventureKEEN

Bailey the bear cub yawns and stretches on her soft bed of pine needles. The sunlight warms her fur. Bailey loves her home in the forest. It is full of all the right things: trees, food, wind, rain, sunshine, and good smells.

Bailey is hungry, and Mama Bear smells something tasty. Bailey walks with her toward the scent. Mama weaves through the trees with her nose in the air, but Bailey finds a wide, flat path.

When Mama turns, she sees Bailey walking on a road! She tries to warn Bailey, but Mama is too late.

CRASH!

A car hits Bailey!

Bailey is alive, but her entire body aches. Her mouth hurts worst of all. She cannot cry or call for help.

Strangers approach her slowly. Bailey can see Mama in the forest, watching her. She is glad that Mama is safe.

The strangers gently wrap a blanket around Bailey and pick her up. They move her into the back of a special truck because Bailey needs help.

When the truck stops moving, the strangers carry Bailey into a building. These strangers are veterinarians. They take X-ray pictures of Bailey's whole body. They talk softly as they look at the images.

Bailey's X-rays show that her jaw is broken. The rest of her body is bruised, but no other bones are broken.

The veterinarians give her medicine, and Bailey falls asleep.

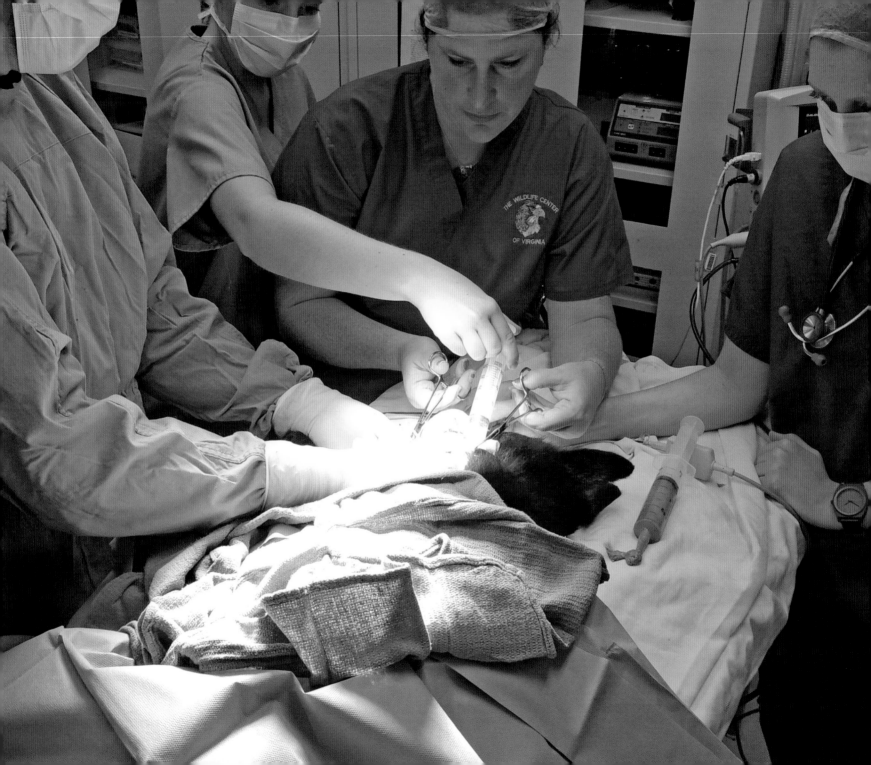

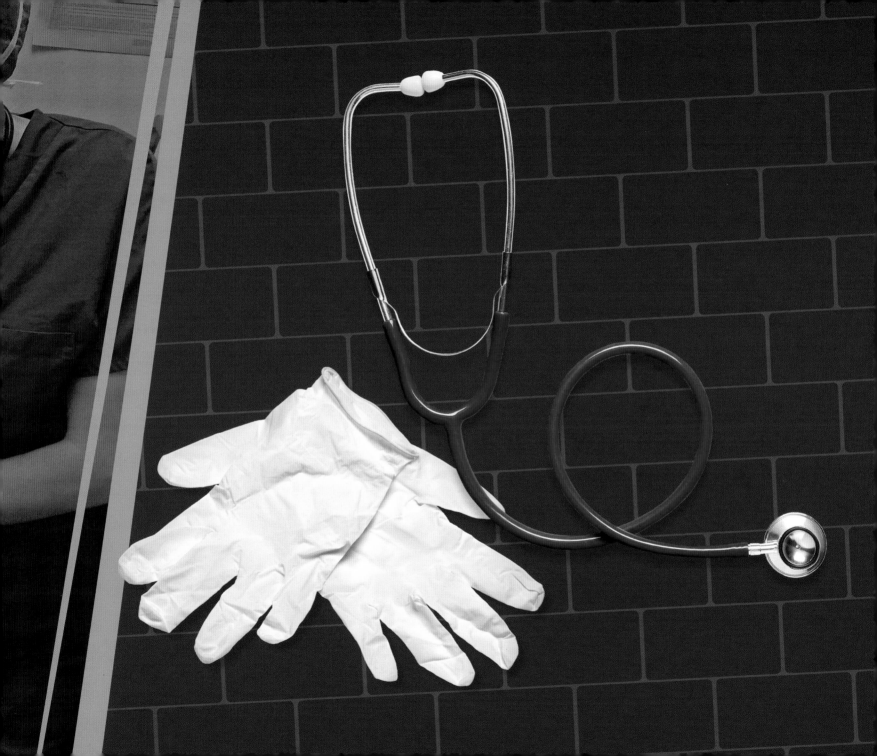

When Bailey wakes up, she hears a veterinarian talking about her face.

"We put metal pins in her jaw, with a hard piece of plaster to hold the jaw in place. This will support her broken jaw while it heals," says the veterinarian.

The plaster feels weird, but Bailey's jaw hurts less.

Bailey is placed in a small box with plastic sides and a soft floor. She is scared, and her body is sore. A veterinarian gives her special medicine, and she is able to fall asleep again.

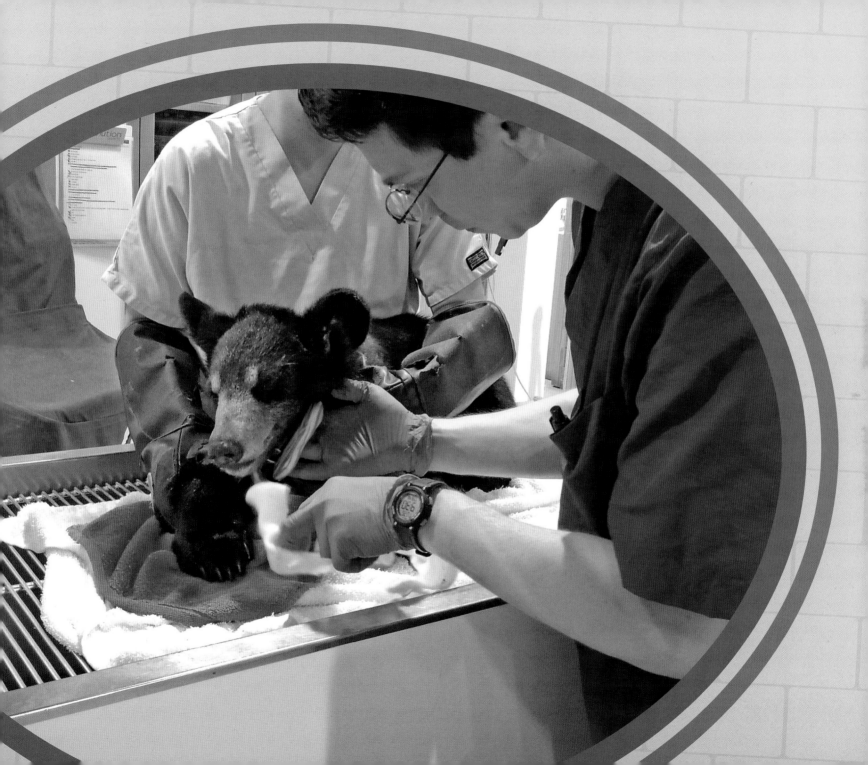

When she opens her eyes, there is a bowl of soft dog food waiting. It smells good. Bailey's stomach growls.

She opens her mouth and takes a bite.

OUCH!

Eating hurts. She stops for a few minutes. But her grumbly tummy wants food, so she tries again.

OUCH again! But also tasty.

After a few days of eating soft food, Bailey is moved to an outdoor area. She can feel the wind and hear the birds. She begins to climb and play.

Someone brings a treat of fresh strawberries.

MUNCH, CHOMP, YUM!

Bailey still has the plaster cast on her face, but she can eat just fine.

A few days later, the veterinarians take new X-ray pictures of Bailey's jaw. When they look at the pictures, they cheer. All the good food, medicine, and fresh air are working. Bailey's jaw is healing.

The veterinarians give her the sleepy medicine again, and they take the plaster cast off her face.

When they bring her food, a veterinarian says, "This is what the big bears eat."

Bailey devours insects, bird seeds, fish, vegetables, and some crunchy bites of dog food. She eats every bite and then takes a long nap.

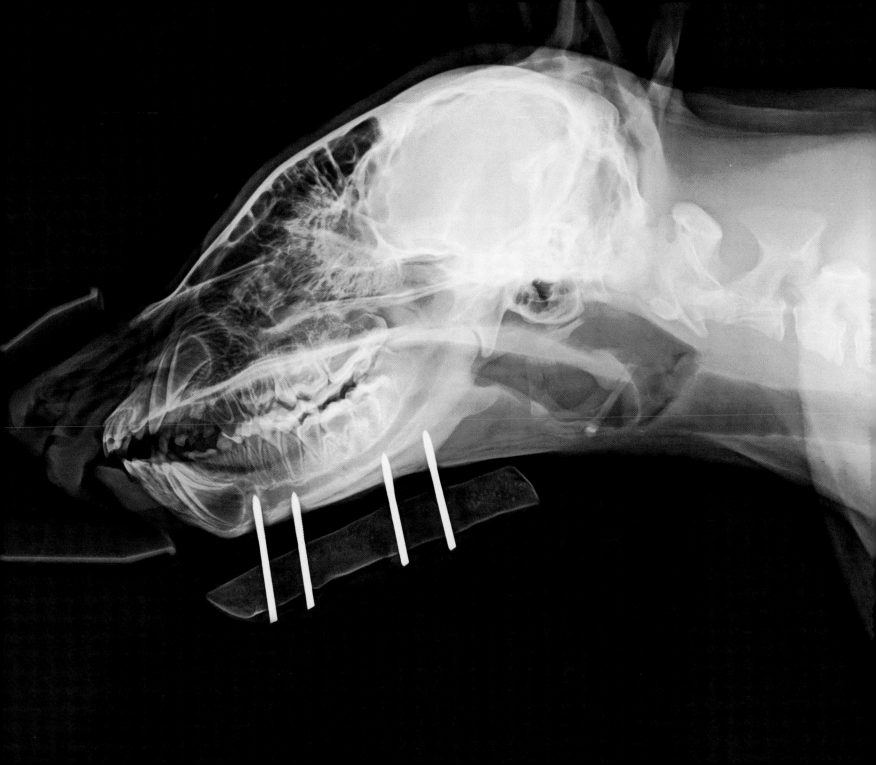

One day, the veterinarians bring Bailey to a different, larger outdoor area. Her heart fills with joy because other injured bears are here, getting better.

The veterinarians tell Bailey that she will live with her new friends as she grows stronger.

Bailey discovers that these friends like to play! They climb trees. They tumble and wrestle. They eat together too.

Bailey gains weight and gets bigger. She stays in this area all winter, playing in the snow and ice with her friends. The veterinarians see that she can take care of herself. It has been almost a year since the accident. Bailey barely remembers it.

One spring day, Bailey and her friends are loaded into a truck.
The veterinarians give them medicine to make them tired.
This keeps them safe during the ride.

When the truck stops, the door opens. There
are no buildings. There are no walls. Instead,
Bailey sees trees and sky. She has a clear
view of the forest—and Bailey remembers.
She remembers her love for the place
where she was born.

Bailey is the first to step out of the truck. She walks away slowly. She lifts her nose and sniffs the fresh air.

Bailey looks over her shoulder at the people who helped her, and she nods at them. Then she starts to run.

She moves into the cool woods, soft pine needles crunching underneath her paws. Bailey the bear is home again.

What kind of bear is Bailey?

Bailey is a black bear. Black bears are the most common bears in North America. They eat nearly everything. They are omnivorous, meaning they eat plants and meat. Bears love insects, seeds, berries, fish, and more! They mostly forage (search the forest) for their food. Bears can be either diurnal (awake in the day) or nocturnal (awake during the night). Even though they look large and slow, bears are excellent runners, swimmers, and climbers.

How do bear cubs stay safe?

From an early age, mama bears teach their cubs to climb trees when danger is near. Bear cubs can't fight a predator, so they use their sharp claws to get off the ground and into a tree. The mama bear will let them know when it is safe to come down.

What happened to Bailey's mom?

When Bailey was hit by the car, her mom and another cub were nearby. They did not get hurt. The rescuers saw them in the woods. Bailey needed help, so she had to be separated from her parent. Bear cubs usually stay with their mother for a year, while they learn to find food and fend for themselves. This is why the wildlife center kept Bailey until the spring. Releasing a young bear in the winter would be difficult because there isn't much food available to eat. Many bears hibernate for several weeks during winter.

What is hibernation?

Hibernation is a way that some animals survive the cold winters, while food is hard to find. When an animal hibernates, it remains inside its home for weeks or months. The animal doesn't sleep the entire time, but it remains dormant, which means it doesn't move very often and its entire body slows way down—including breathing rate and heartbeat. This helps the animal to save energy over a long period of time, so it doesn't need to eat. Not many animals are able to hibernate, but some hibernators include certain types of bats, chipmunks, snails, snakes, and turtles.

Do bears really hibernate?

Not exactly. Most people say that bears hibernate, but what they actually do is called "torpor." It comes close to hibernation, but torpor is a much lighter dormant state, meaning the animals' bodies don't slow down nearly as much. Bears eat a lot in preparation for torpor. During torpor, their body temperature drops, so they burn less energy. They breathe very slowly, and their heartbeat slows too. They may only change body positions every couple of days. They do not eat, drink, or pass waste (pee or poop) during torpor—sometimes longer than 100 days! Bears in very cold climates are more likely to remain in torpor all winter. Bears in warmer climates will sometimes wake from their winter naps for a little while to grab a snack when the temperature rises.

How do bears find a den?

Bears often dig their own dens. Sometimes they use brush piles, hollow trees, caves, or other animals' old dens. The bear will cover the floor with pine needles or other soft forest material. These floor coverings help to hold heat and keep the bear from sleeping on the cold ground. Bears start to get very sleepy in the late fall. They often enter their dens during the first big snowfall of winter. The theory is that perhaps the snowfall will cover their tracks and hide the entrance of the den. That's pretty smart! If a female bear is pregnant, the cubs will be born inside the den, midwinter. They sleep next to their mother and nurse from her while she sleeps.

What if a bear is getting into our garbage or bird feeder?

Move the trash bin into a garage or shed for a few days. And when you leave it outside, close the lid with a cord or strap so the bear can't open it. If the bear loses its food source, it should stop coming. For bird feeders, take them inside for a few days. This also encourages the bear to move along and find other food sources. If bears get used to eating human food (from garbage cans, bird feeders, or even litter), they end up being around humans too often, which puts their lives at risk. A bear that is comfortable around humans can get into dangerous situations.

What if I see a bear cub that's all alone?

Stay away! Even if a bear cub seems alone, its mother is most likely nearby—and we don't want to separate her from her cub if no help is needed. Plus, all wild animals, even baby animals, can be dangerous to pick up. If you are worried about the cub—or any animal that seems hurt or in danger—have an adult call a wildlife rehabilitation center. The trained experts will know what to do. You should never go near a wild animal.

Tell me more about the wildlife rehabilitation (rehab) centers.

Wildlife rehab centers and wildlife hospitals care for all types of animals. Their goal is to help each animal get better and return to the wild. The animals are treated by veterinarians and teams of experts who specialize in this work. Sometimes animals need surgery, like Bailey did! Sometimes they need medicine, also like Bailey. Sometimes they need food and support to get stronger. Bailey's journey through the wildlife center shows what these specialized hospitals can do for wild animals.

How can I help?

By buying this book, you are helping. Part of the proceeds are donated to the wildlife center that helped Bailey. You can also help by donating directly to your local wildlife rehab center! And you can help bears by cleaning up your trash at home—and when you are out in nature.

This book is dedicated to the Wildlife Center of Virginia. Every day, the people here work to rescue and rehabilitate native wildlife. Their devotion to wildlife and their commitment to the ongoing education of adults and children is evident in everything they do. They have supplied stories, photos, and support throughout the writing and publication of the Wildlife Rescue Stories.

In particular, I want to thank Amanda Nicholson for her guidance and support. Her expertise has been invaluable. Amanda is a dedicated, enthusiastic, and passionate educator. I am so lucky to have met her. Thank you, Amanda!

Photo Credits by Photographer and Page Number
Front cover: Curly Pat/Shutterstock.com (background pattern); Michel VIARD/iStock.com (bear cub climbing); Wildlife Center of Virginia (inset)

Spine: jadimages/Shutterstock.com

Back cover: Geoffrey Kuchera/Shutterstock.com (Bear on Rock); Holly Kuchera/Shutterstock.com (inset); Curly Pat/Shutterstock.com (background pattern)

Peter Gove: 32 (author photo); Wildlife Center of Virginia: 7 (bear), 10, 11 (both), 12, 15, 17 (bear), 18, 20 (food bowl), 21, 22, 23, 26 (both), 29, 30, 31

Images used under license from Shutterstock.com: Galyna Andrushko: 5 (bear cub), 6 (bear cub), 7 (green background); cobalt88: 27 (trees); Curly Pat: (background patterns) 2, 3, 7, 8, 10, 12, 14, 16, 19, 20, 22, 26, 29, 32; Ghost Bear: 2; Ivgroznii: 4-5 (background pattern); Jadimages: 28; Susan Kehoe: 9 (bear); Alexey Kljatov: 24 (snowflakes); Malenkka: 7 (asphalt), 9 (asphalt); Julia Moiseenko: 25; David Osborn: 4 (bear); Phoenix45photo: 8; pics five: 13 (gloves); PitchyPix: 17 (dog food); Pixel-Shot: 13 (stethoscope); Prystai: 9 (blanket); Anton Starikov: 3 (pine needles); Supergenijalac: 6 (car); Alex Zaitsev: 24 (snow background).

Edited by Ryan Jacobson; cover and book design by Jonathan Norberg
10 9 8 7 6 5 4 3 2 1
Bailey the Bear Needs Help!
Copyright © 2023 by Christy Gove
Published by Adventure Publications, an imprint of AdventureKEEN
310 Garfield Street South, Cambridge, Minnesota 55008, (800) 678-7006
www.adventurepublications.net
All rights reserved. Printed in China
Cataloging-in-Publication data is available from the Library of Congress
ISBN 978-1-64755-344-9 (pbk); ISBN 978-1-64755-345-6 (ebook)

About the Author

Christy Gove is the author of five books, including *Maggie the One-Eyed Peregrine Falcon*, *Greta the Great Horned Owl*, *Minnesota Must-See for Families*, and *Bailey the Bear Needs Help!* Her first book, *Esther the Eaglet*, was inspired by an eagle rescue that took place at her parent's cabin. From that experience, she learned about the unique and important work done by wildlife rehabilitation hospitals. The experience inspired her to research and write about more animal rescue stories. Christy lives just outside Minnesota's Twin Cities. She enjoys spending time in nature, especially hiking, kayaking, and camping. She is the parent to three amazing kids and goes adventuring with them as often as possible.